09

The Legend of Blue Jacket

by Michael P. Spradlin 🌿 illustrated by Ronald Himler

HarperCollinsPublishers

To Kelly, Mike Jr., and Rachel, with love

The Legend of Blue Jacket
Text copyright © 2002 by Michael P. Spradlin
Illustrations copyright © 2002 by Ronald Himler
Manufactured in China. All rights reserved.
www.harperchildrens.com

Library of Congress Cataloging-in-Publication Data
Spradlin, Michael P.
   The legend of Blue Jacket / by Michael P. Spradlin ; illustrated by Ronald Himler.
      p.   cm.
   ISBN 0-688-15835-8 — ISBN 0-688-15836-6 (lib. bdg.)
   1. Blue Jacket, b. ca. 1752. 2. Shawnee Indians—Biography—Juvenile literature. 3. Indian captivities—Ohio—Juvenile literature. 4. Shawnee Indians—Wars, 1775–1883—Juvenile literature. I. Himler, Ronald, ill. II. Title.
E99.S35 B587 2002   2001024749
974.004'973—dc21   CIP
                                                                                                      AC

Typography by Robbin Gourley and Jeanne Hogle
2 3 4 5 6 7 8 9 10

First Edition

Preface

This is the story of a historical figure whose life, not unlike Robin Hood's or George Washington's, has become clouded in myth, exaggeration, and controversy. The stories in *The Legend of Blue Jacket* are drawn from my own twelve-year study of the history of the people and places of the eighteenth-century Ohio River valley. To my mind, it is one of the richest but least known periods of the American past.

Blue Jacket, the Shawnee war chief, left no diaries or personal records of any kind. This book is based on studies of documents, books, journals, and other accounts of the period, many of which are catalogued in the archives of the State Historical Society of Wisconsin. The Draper Collection, housed there, is a treasure trove of information on the history of this period, but sadly it contains very little original source material that pertains to Blue Jacket. While there is no first-person account of Marmaduke Van Swearingen's capture, I did read more than twenty first-person accounts of white settlers captured by the Shawnee and other Ohio tribes, and I believe the events as depicted here are an accurate re-creation. In addition, I have also studied numerous volumes on the history and culture of Ohio River valley tribes. Most useful was the book *Shawnee: The Ceremonialism of a Native American Tribe and Its Cultural Background* by James Howard.

In recent years, there has been great discussion about whether Blue Jacket and Marmaduke Van Swearingen were the same man. Many respected historians have weighed in on both sides of the issue. Confusion over the dates of Van Swearingen's birth, the first reference to a Shawnee named Blue Jacket in the historical record, and the veracity of several documents and eyewitness accounts—which historians argue prove the case one way or the other—have all become objects of dispute.

Many of the historians who claim that Marmaduke Van Swearingen was not Blue Jacket use as their central argument the idea that an Indian tribe would never allow a white captive to rise to the position of war chief. This seems an ethnocentric viewpoint to me and shows a lack of understanding of the Shawnee culture.

From the time the first Europeans landed on American shores, thousands of men, women, and children were captured by Indians or escaped indentured servitude to live with Indian tribes across the nation. Many lived their entire lives as Native Americans and never returned to the white world. The historical record is filled with hundreds of accounts of white captives who became influential members of their adoptive tribes. Numerous French and British traders and soldiers were given tribal memberships, wielded great influence with Indians, and at times led raiding parties against their enemies.

Further, except in time of war, the Shawnee war chief held no influence over the tribe in social, cultural, or political matters. Blue Jacket figures prominently in this period only because from 1774 to 1794 the Shawnee were in a state of near constant war.

From all that I have read and studied, I believe that Marmaduke Van Swearingen was born in 1753 and was captured by the Shawnee in the spring of 1769. Beginning in 1774, Blue Jacket starts becoming a prominent figure in the history of that era. The exact date of Blue Jacket's death has never been determined, but there is so little reference to him after 1810 that I believe this must be the year he died. Very few of the events of Blue Jacket's life can be proven as absolute, most of all during his early years, but there is an overwhelming amount of anecdotal information, oral history, and circumstantial evidence that convinces me that Marmaduke Van Swearingen became Blue Jacket. Yet whether he was a white man or Native American is less important than the legacy he left behind in the green forests of Ohio.

$\mathcal{A}$mong the People I am called Blue Jacket, but that was not always my name. I came to live with the People when I was a young man. Before I became Blue Jacket, my name was Duke Van Swearingen.

My American family were soldiers and farmers. When I was a small boy, we moved to the western part of Virginia and farmed. I loved living near the forest, and my father taught my three brothers, my sister, and me the ways of the woods. Father spent many hours teaching us all he knew about the Indian tribes that lived nearby—the Delaware, Mingo, Miami, and Shawnee. From him we learned some Indian words, and he told us always to be careful and alert when we were in the forest.

Life with my family on the frontier was hard and rugged. Whenever I could, I escaped to the woods near our farm to hunt and fish. As I walked the forest, I dreamed of exploring the vast wilderness that lay to the west of our land.

When I was about to turn sixteen, I had the chance to live my dream. On a cold, clear spring day, I went with my younger brother, Charlie, to the wooded hills

above our farm to help him look for herbs for our mother to use in cooking. I was wearing a blue linsey-woolsey jacket to keep warm. For a moment we stopped to rest beneath a tall maple tree. In less than three heartbeats, we were surrounded by a group of Indians. They did not wear war paint, yet they looked ferocious, and at first I was scared. Then I remembered that my father had told me that Indians admired courage above all else, and I tried not to show any fear. Quietly, I laid my walking stick on the ground and held out my empty palms.

My brother was afraid, and I did my best to comfort him. The Indians studied us for many minutes, and finally the man who seemed to be their leader reached out to touch the blue jacket that I wore. He pointed to us and said, "Shemanese." Then he pointed to himself and said, "Shawanese." Then he pointed to himself again and said, "Pucksinwah." He made a sign for Charlie and me to come with him. My brother began to cry.

I tried to make Pucksinwah understand that I would go with him peacefully if he would let Charlie stay. It took a long time to make him understand. Finally Pucksinwah smiled and nodded.

I gave Charlie a fierce hug and mounted a horse behind one of Pucksinwah's men. My heart was pounding in my chest. I was a little afraid, but a part of me was excited too. I was finally going to see the land I had always wondered about.

For many days I traveled with Pucksinwah and his band. As I rode with the

Shawnee, I learned a few of their words. For the first few days we rode hard, through streams and creeks, not leaving any tracks for a search party to follow. At night we lit no fires and slept close to the horses. Finally, we crested a mountain ridge, and below us lay the sparkling surface of the Ohio River. It was the biggest river I had ever seen. It surged through the green carpet of the forest and wound its way westward until it disappeared beyond our sight.

Pucksinwah led us along the shore of the river to a place where several canoes

had been filled with stones and hidden beneath the water. The warriors soon
had the canoes afloat, and we climbed in while part of the group herded the horses
across the river. After crossing the river, we rested awhile.

After a few more hours of riding, we came to Pucksinwah's village. I was taken
to the center of the village and saw a startling sight. Stretched out before me for
hundreds of yards were villagers in two lines, facing one another. All of them held

sticks, clubs, and switches cut from tree branches. I had heard my father speak of what happened to prisoners in Shawnee towns. I was going to run the gauntlet.

Pucksinwah took my blue jacket off me and held it aloft, waving it about his head. From his gestures I figured that he was telling the people about my capture. Then he turned to me. In broken English and with simple signs, Pucksinwah told me that I would have to run the gauntlet. I was to run as fast as I could toward a log house at the end of the line, and the People would try to hit me with the switches and clubs as I ran by. It was a test of my courage. If I passed, I would be considered for adoption into the tribe.

I waited for Pucksinwah's club to strike. He hit me a stunning blow across the back, and I staggered down the line. Immediately the People fell upon me, their clubs and switches flailing me like the beating wings of the raven. I ran as fast as I could, trying to pass as many people as possible. Many times I fell, and their blows rained down on me. Yet somehow I kept going. Finally I collapsed across the entrance to the log house, battered and bleeding.

For several weeks I lay in a hut, scarcely able to move. Women from the village took care of me. They packed my wounds with buzzard down and coated the welts and scratches on my skin with bear grease. These women also helped me learn more Shawnee words.

I lived with the People for many months, and gradually I grew more comfortable with their way of life.

One night, Pucksinwah came to visit me in my wigewa. We talked long into the night about what I had seen and learned during my time with the People. Finally, he asked me, "Blue Jacket, do you wish to stay with us?" He smiled when I replied in the Shawnee language, "The heart of Blue Jacket is now a Shawnee heart."

The next day I was painted with many different colors and dressed in deerskin trousers. A great chief named Black Fish, who was to be my adoptive father, came to my wigewa and led me through the village, down to the river. I walked into the river as all of the villagers watched. Some women followed me into the water and scrubbed the paint from my skin with pebbles and sand. When all the paint was gone, Black Fish told everyone that my white blood had been washed away in the river, that I was now one of the People, and that I would live among them with all the rights of a Shawnee. When Black Fish said, "We welcome our brother Blue Jacket," the People cheered.

My life among the People really began that day. In the months that followed, I learned more of the Shawnee language. I would listen for hours as Black Fish, Pucksinwah, and our great chief, Cornstalk, told me the stories of the Shawnee. They spoke of how the People were created by Moneto the

Creator. When the People were hungry, Moneto sent Corn Woman and Pumpkin Woman to feed us. Black Fish also patiently explained my obligations as a Shawnee warrior. It was my duty to serve and protect the People, even if it meant sacrificing my own life.

Black Fish and Pucksinwah spent many hours telling me about the threat of the Americans, the Shemanese. The Shawnee leaders believed that war was coming, and as a warrior I must fight the Americans, never trust them, and keep the People safe from them. They felt the Americans would soon build wigewas in the sacred Caintuckee hunting grounds. Already warriors had found white settlers traveling through Caintuckee, hunting game and building small cabins. The warriors would drive them out and tell them not to come back, yet more would return. Many times the American hunters and trappers would kill our warriors, and our parties would return in mourning. I began to wonder why the Americans were not willing to share the country as we did with the Delaware, the Mingo, and other tribes. When I would see our warriors return with dead and wounded brothers, it made me sad and angry.

Our villages depended on the warriors to hunt and bring us food. Since I had spent many hours practicing with the bow and musket, I became an excellent hunter and marksman. One day Black Fish decided that I could join them in their raids against the Americans. We traveled south, to the Caintuckee hunting grounds. When we came upon parties of Americans, we took their furs and horses and

ordered them to leave. Yet there were so many of them and so few of us that no matter how many we sent away, more came to fill their places. But I began to relish these adventures and soon drew praise from the chiefs for my skills as a warrior.

In my village there was a pretty, young woman who, like me, was born an American. I soon found myself making excuses to see her. The village women did all they could to bring us together at dances and feasts. We soon fell in love and were married, and after that our son Joseph was born. I had never felt so happy.

In the year the Americans called 1774, Cornstalk sent messengers to the governor of Virginia, Lord Dunmore, to ask him to stop his people from coming to Caintuckee. Lord Dunmore would not agree to this. He said instead that if the Shawnee harmed any more of his people, he would send his army to punish us.

Cornstalk knew that the Virginians were strong. In council, he advised the Shawnee and our brothers the Miami, the Delaware, and the Mingo that we should make a new treaty with the Virginians, that to fight them was foolish. But the People had their hearts set on war. We would sign no treaty.

We met the Shemanese at a place they called Point Pleasant. We knew that we had caught them in a bad place, but they fought bravely.

When the battle at Point Pleasant was over, neither side could claim victory. We

had killed many Americans, but they had killed our warriors in nearly equal numbers. My Shawnee brothers told me that I had fought well. Cornstalk found me after the fighting was over and told me he was proud of me. But he also had terrible news: Pucksinwah had died in the battle.

His words were a flame in my heart, but I vowed to be brave and keep fighting. Pucksinwah's spirit would live on in all of us.

As Cornstalk had advised us before the battle, we signed a new treaty with the

Virginians. This treaty said that the Shawnee and other tribes had no rights to the Caintuckee lands. We could hunt, and gather salt there, but we could not harm the settlers. The treaty changed my life forever. It said that all white persons who were captives of the Shawnee must be returned to their homes. Since I had come to live with the People on my own, I was free. But my wife would have to go back to her American family.

When the soldiers came to take our families, my wife and I could not speak for the grief that filled our hearts. I held her close to me and could scarcely bear to let her go.

Our son would stay with me. He was too small to make the trip, and he would be raised a Shawnee. I watched my wife mount a horse and join the women and children who were going back to the Americans. Standing on a hill outside the village, I gazed at her until she rode beyond my sight. I never saw her again.

The new treaty brought many more settlers to Caintuckee. One of the men who came to Caintuckee was a great warrior named Daniel Boone. The Shawnee fought against Boone in many battles, but we could never defeat him. He seemed to be blessed by Moneto. Because he was short and compact, we called him Shelowotee, which means Big Turtle.

One day Black Fish and I led a party of warriors to Caintuckee. We were going to a place called Blue Licks. It was a natural salt lick, where we would gather salt

for cooking and preserving food. As we made our way there, we came upon a man alone in the woods. It was Shelowotee—Boone.

Boone tried to run away, but I rode after him and captured him before he could escape. I told Boone that he must tell his party to lay down their guns, that he and his men should come peacefully with us to our village. Boone finally agreed when I promised that his people would be kept safe and would not be forced to run the gauntlet. He went into their camp and told the settlers that it was useless to fight. We took the prisoners to our village.

Capturing Big Turtle made me a great hero to the People. Just as I had been, Boone was later adopted into the tribe as a Shawnee. For many months we lived and hunted together, and I taught Boone some of the Shawnee language.

During the time that Big Turtle lived with the People, the Americans went to war against their English king. The English soldiers came to our villages and promised us great riches if we would make war against the Americans. Black Fish told the Redcoats that we would strike the white towns in Caintuckee in the spring. When Boone learned of our plans, he waited for the right moment and sneaked away from us in time to warn the settlers of the Shawnee attack.

The Shawnee soon joined the fight with our English brothers against our sworn enemies, the Americans. It was not an easy decision to join the war, and many of the People felt that we could not stop the Americans. The Shawnee who did not wish to

fight anymore decided to leave Ohio forever. They went west beyond the mother of all rivers, the Mississippi, to live away from the Americans, to find peace. The heart of the People was broken forever. Those of us who stayed behind vowed to die before giving up our homes.

The war with the Americans went on for many years. We fought against Boone and the great Long Knife, George Rogers Clark, and took many scalps. Once during

the war I found myself in Caintuckee, near Boonesboro, where Big Turtle made his home. In the woods nearby I was tracking horses that had been stolen from us by the Americans. Suddenly I was surrounded by Caintuckians. Though I had not spoken American words in many years, I made them understand that I was a friend of Boone, and they took me to him.

When Big Turtle looked at me, I knew he realized that his men would surely kill me if they knew who I was. After thinking for a few minutes, he told them to tie my hands, and he led us to a small log hut. Boone made a show of making sure my hands were tied securely and told his men to post a guard. Later that night I heard the guard outside begin to snore. I struggled against the ropes but could not free myself. Then a shuttered window at the back of the hut opened, and I saw the face of my friend Boone.

Quickly Boone reached through the window and stuck a small hunting knife in one of the logs of the hut. Then he was gone. When I thought it was safe, I cut my bonds with the knife and escaped. Boone had not forgotten his friend Blue Jacket.

Our fights against the Americans never ceased. We tried to push them out of Caintuckee, but we could not get rid of them. One day word came to our villages that the Americans had defeated our English brothers and that their war was over. Our hearts became like stones. We knew the war's end meant that even more Americans would come to Caintuckee.

Though the English and American war was over, our war was not. In the early years after the Revolution, my greatest day with the People took place. In a ceremony before the Shawnee nation, Black Hoof and Moluntha, our chiefs, called out my name. As I stood before them, they asked if I would become the Maykujay chief of the Shawnee. This meant that I would lead the People in war and defend them with my life and with the lives of my Shawnee brothers. My heart swelled with pride. I stood before the council fire and spoke to the People.

Before the council fire were two log posts. One had been painted white for peace and one red for war. I took out my tomahawk and buried it in the red war pole.

As the People let out a thunderous shout, I danced around the war pole, bathed in the light of the council fire. For a brief moment, I thought of how far I had come since the day I left Duke Van Swearingen behind. I have lived a Shawnee life of honor and service to Moneto and the People. I have been a man of two worlds, but nothing will make me wish I had stayed in my old life. I am Blue Jacket, war chief of the Shawnee. That will forever be my name.

Afterword

As war chief of the Shawnee, Blue Jacket must surely be considered one of the greatest military leaders in Native American history. Warriors commanded by Blue Jacket nearly destroyed the army of General Arthur St. Clair. In that battle the United States army suffered the worst defeat ever at the hands of Native Americans, with Indian forces inflicting nearly four times as many casualties as in the more famous Battle of the Little Big Horn some eighty years later.

Blue Jacket and his coalition of tribes were finally defeated by General "Mad" Anthony Wayne at the Battle of Fallen Timbers in 1794. Even then the battle was close and the outcome long undecided. Some historians speculate that if Blue Jacket had been given the British aid he had been promised, he would have defeated Wayne. The following year Blue Jacket signed the Treaty of Greenville and never again took up arms against the United States. The exact date of his death is not known. It has been given as early as 1810 and as late as 1824.

Blue Jacket's first wife was a white captive named Margaret Moore. Unknown to Blue Jacket, his wife was pregnant with his daughter when she was returned to Virginia. Nancy Blue Jacket first saw her father in the early 1800s. She had four children, none of whom married.

Blue Jacket did marry again and fathered several more children. One of Blue Jacket's sons, Jim Blue Jacket, became a trusted lieutenant of Tecumseh and joined his effort to unite all of the eastern tribes against white settlement on Indian lands. After Tecumseh's death in 1814 at the Battle of the Thames, most of the remaining Ohio Shawnee went west to live with the so-called Absentee Shawnee near what is now Shawnee Mission, Kansas. By 1832 all Shawnee still living in the Great Lakes area had been moved to Kansas. Many of the Absentee Shawnee who moved west were then forced to give up their lands in Kansas and move to Oklahoma's Indian territory, far away from Blue Jacket's beloved Ohio country.